UNDERSTANDING FEELINGS OF LOVE

Encouragement and Inspiration with Short Stories by Teens and Young Adults

Jennifer Leigh Youngs, A.A. • Bettie B. Youngs, Ph.D., Ed.D.

from the SMART TEENS-SMART CHOICES series

Teen Town Press
www.TeenTownPress.com

an imprint of Bettie Youngs Book Publishers, Inc.

Cover Graphic Design: Adrian Pitariu and Beau Kimbrel
Text Design: Beau Kimbrel
Teen Consultant: Kendahl Brooke Youngs

TEEN TOWN PRESS / www.TeenTownPress.com is an Imprint of Bettie Youngs Book Publishing Co., Inc.: www.BettieYoungsBooks.com; info@BettieYoungsBooks.com.

If you are unable to order this book from your local bookseller or online, or Ingram Book Group, you may order directly from the publisher: info@BettieYoungsBooks.com.

PRINT ISBN: 978-1-940784-75-5
DIGITAL ISBN: 978-1-940784-74-8

10 9 8 7 6 5 4 3 2

Library of Congress Cataloging-in-Publication Data Available upon Request.

Summary: Information and encouragement on understanding feelings of love, with inspirational short stories by teens and young adults.
1. YAN literature. 2. Love. 3. Virtues. 4. Teens and Young Adults. 5. Relationships. 6. Values. 7. Friendships. 8. Confidence. 9. Self-esteem. 10. Emotions. 11. Youngs, Bettie Burres. 12. Youngs, Jennifer Leigh.

Also by the Authors for Teens and Young Adults

How Your Brain Decides If You Will Become Addicted—Or Not

Setting and Achieving Goals that Matter TO ME

Managing the Stress, Pressure and the Ups and Downs of Life

The 10 Commandments and the Secret Each One Guards—FOR YOU

How to Be Courageous

Growing Your Confidence and Self-Esteem

Faith at Work in Our Lives

Understanding Feelings of Love

Understanding the Christian Faith

How to be a Good Friend

Having Healthy and Beautiful Hair, Skin and Nails

The Power of Being Kind, Courteous and Thoughtful

How to Have a Great Attitude

Caring for Your Body's Health and Wellness

Daily Inspiration

Inspirational Stories and Encouragement on Friends and the Face in the Mirror

CONTENTS

    - Understanding Feelings
    - The Power of Love in Our Lives
    - Learning to be a Loving Person
    - Who was Your FIRST LOVE?

- A Tete-a-Tete with Your Heart
- "How Far Will You Go" for Love?
- Someone Special in Your Life
- Mending a Broken Heart

CHAPTER 1
EXPRESSIONS OF LOVE

"I love you": three little words that hold a lot of meaning, and power.

Love. Just saying the word conjures up a sense of wonderment, of joie de vivre—an exciting feeling that fills life with elation and joy. It's so important to feel love—and express it.

It's been said that we need at least one hug a day to survive, two to be healthy, three to be a happy person and four to feel loved. Love is more than just hugs of course, but the point is that we all need love.

Maybe the need to feel loved, and to give love, is built into our genes, or as teen Amanda Mossor says in her story in Chapter Two, "We're 'coded' for love." Maybe that's why we seek love: We need it to be happy and healthy.

Love is the most potent force in all the world, says as the great philosopher Teilhard de Chardin. The supremacy of its power is what prompted his remark: "*Someday, after we master the winds, the waves, the tides and gravity, we shall harness the energies of love. Then, for the second time in the history of the world, man will have discovered fire.*"

What greater force for good, what greater depth

1

of emotion exists, what greater gift could one give or receive, what gift is more priceless, than love? Perhaps none!

Love is the major task we are charged with in our lifetimes—to come from our hearts, to lead with our hearts, and to use out love wisely.

One thing is for sure, when it comes to matters of love, many young adults lead with their hearts.

> "We need at least one hug a day to survive, two to be healthy, three to be a happy person and four to feel loved."

The Heart, the Symbol for Love

The heart represents love, and in turn, the symbol for love is the shape of a heart. The very image of a heart conjures up feelings of tenderness, affection and caretaking. Love, feelings and actions motivated by giving and receiving from the heart, is an essential emotion necessary to the well-being of our lives.

With love in our lives we can see more clearly the beauty and potential within ourselves, and in others, too.

That we can give love speaks to the miraculous definition of the human heart to seek what it needs, time and time again. Even in cases where the heart loses a love, or rejects one because it isn't right for us, it begins a new search; our hearts are on a constant quest for love.

As the saying goes, *"LOVE makes the world go 'round"*!

No writing is more inspired than a love letter, or even a "let's make up" letter. For that matter, even the "get-lost" letter in love's demise.

Ah! Love letters! Imagine the letters we've sent that should have never been sent, the ones we've written and never sent (but wished we had), the ones we wished we'd written, and the ones we've received and those we've saved for years! Whether you write them because you're burning with the desire to express your passion, or to say you're "done," writing them is a powerful way to communicate!

Your stories and poetry proves that love inspires creativity! You said love was definitely on your mind, and the letters you shared confirm that when it comes to love, Romeo and Juliet have nothing on you. Whether it was to let your girl or guy know it was over, or to ask for another chance, whether you wanted to profess your eternal passion, or to ask your loved one to go steady—or to marry you, your stories speak volumes about how seriously you take feelings of love.

Learning what love means to you, and to others, and finding the boundaries that make love a healthy two-way street for those involved, are only a few of the lessons found in the exploration of love.

As you awaken to feelings of love beyond that of self, family and best friends, you are convinced that love is the point of life! Which is why love cannot only make the world go 'round, but in some cases, can make your life seem as though it's spinning out of control! Alas, Henry David Thoreau was right, *"The heart is forever inexperienced when it comes to matters of love!"*

Making the world go 'round, or spinning out of control, either way, love changes things. Teens and young adults across the country shared stories of love's transforming power, and how it changed or touched their lives, and the lives of others, too.

You even identified love as a powerful catalyst for transforming our homes and communities into places where peace and a sense of community is the standard for how we share our lives, and our earth home, with each other. How insightful!

Your poetry and your letters proved that love, whether taking place only in fantasy or in a "steady" relationship, has the power to give people, young and old, dreams for the future—dreams of connection and passion, romance and greater meaning in life. And they showed that love adds new dimension and brightness to your days, which you deeply value—so much so, that you sometimes have trouble letting go, even when you know it's the illusion of love, more than real love, that you are holding onto. So much so, that you are able to forgive, and able to beg forgiveness and feel just awful when you've made a mistake and hurt love.

So much so, that even when you cringe or blush as you look back at some of the crazy things you've said and done in the name of love, you then do it all over again when you're in love once more!

In addition to all the heart and passion that the following expressions of love communicate, many of them also help prove you're not alone when it comes to literally "going crazy" over your latest love—which is always a nice thing to know.

The teens and young adults hope you're "crazy in love" with the following expressions of love!

CHAPTER 2

STORIES BY TEENS AND YOUNG ADULTS: "WHAT I'VE LEARNED ABOUT LOVE (SO FAR)"

Coded For Love

It wasn't until recently that I realized there is more than one kind of love. I used to drive myself crazy trying to figure out how I could be in love with my boyfriend, but then be instantly attracted to someone else, too. Well, I've finally gotten it figured out. You see, there are different kinds of love. For example, there is love, as in family; love, as in best friends; love, as in first love; love, as in being excited about something; love, as in crush; and love, as in infatuation, to name just a few.

As I see it, these different kinds of love are divided into three categories:

❤ **Category 1: Obligatory Love**

Love for family: This sounds simple enough, but it's really very complicated. Everybody in your family is different, and they each want individual things. And, their motivation for getting them varies. You have to figure out each person in your family if you're going to make the most of family love or else these people will get on your nerves. I've also discovered that you never really know how much you love each person, especially your mom and dad—until you are away for a long trip and get a chance to be lonely. That's when you realize you love them and need their love way more than you think you do.

Love for best friends: You have to really step out on the line and go the distance for your friends. Being on the outs with your best friend hurts about as much as breaking up with a boyfriend. So you really have to learn how to be fair, listen a lot and be willing to let this person in on things you normally wouldn't tell someone else. I could not even imagine my life without my best friend! She's the one person who helps me survive from Monday through Friday, lets me know what others are thinking about me; covers my back and clues me in on things. She is the person who opens her heart to me whenever I need it. (Love for regular friends is not the same as love for best friends—whether they are the same sex as you or not.) **Note:** It's especially important not to accidentally fall in love with a best friend, because why waste a good friendship?

Love, as in being excited about something: Everyone's most likely been in love with something. For instance, I *love* to dance. I dream of dancing being a backup dancer someday for a great band.

❤ **Category 2: Definitely Love (or Sure Feels Like It)**

Puppy love: Who can ever forget that? In fifth grade, it's being in love with every boy in your elementary school class (at least once) and sobbing when the pick of the week checks "no" on the note you pass him. In sixth grade it's being in love with every boy in your class, and knowing if one checks "no" you can always give your note to your second, third or fourth choice.

First love: Now this is the most unforgettable love there is. You could fall in love a hundred-plus times, and yet never, ever experience that wonderful feeling of a *first* love. When you've experienced love for the first time, you've been irrevocably changed! From that moment on, "love" is never an option, it's an absolute necessity—like air or water. First love is the one you spend countless hours dreaming about. This is the person you are absolutely, positively forever sure that your life will never be the same without. This is also the one who leaves you with a horrible empty feeling when he breaks things off with you (or vice versa).

Love, as in crush: A glance, a smile and suddenly: *He's the one!* Now you look forward to going to school, and when he's even in the nearby vicinity, you giggle, laugh and say silly and stupid things even though you once promised yourself you'd never act so dumb. And, of course, you now have to keep tabs on all the girls around, in case they decide they have a crush on your Mr. potential-for-a-first-kiss. You spend hours doodling his initials next to yours, eventually you learn it was only a crush. Nothing more.

Love, as in "geographically undesirable" (GU): Will he ever be mine? You try not to fall for him because he lives so far away, goes to a rival school, is a movie star, or has body "art" your parents won't approve of. In your eyes, what's keeping you two from being the next Romeo and Juliet is only a matter of time, space and perspective. (Not that this can demolish the hopes of your being together some day.) All and all, this love is pretty much ill-fated and never becomes anything more than just a prolonged crush, but at least it's easier on your heart when you realize it's over.

Love, as in infatuation: Ohmygosh! He's so hot! It's that one with the trendy hair, great eyes, a killer smile. The star football player asks you, YES YOU, out. Then you realize you've spent all this time admiring "the football star" and never taken time out to meet the real him. Unfortunately, he is hardly ever the guy you thought he would be. For such a winner on the football field, he doesn't score many points when it comes to loving you as much as he loves himself—nor for spending as much time with you as he does with football and his friends. But you are so in love with his exterior that it's not until your best friend (because she's tired of hearing you complain) makes you realize he's no good for you, that you grudgingly dump him. (After all, being seen with him has its perks.)

❤ Category 3: True Love

Love, as in true love: True love is the one you thank your lucky stars for. It is what almost every person in the world seeks in life. I've been told that true love makes an already complete person even more complete. Poets write poems about it, musicians write songs about it, artists are moved to create masterpieces because of it. True love is destined, fated, meant to be. **Note:** A few of the other loves might also inspire such artistic tributes, so you can't count on this alone to prove that you have found true love.

So you see, love truly is a complicated feeling, no matter which category or what kind it is. The thing is, we humans are probably just coded for love. And that's why if you don't get it right the first time, you just keep working your way through the list. So if you don't get it right, you need to just decide to overcome your heartaches and give love another chance somewhere else, with someone else.

Really, there's enough love to go around. There isn't a person alive who isn't feeling love somewhere, somehow, with someone—and, hopefully it begins with feeling love for themselves.

—Amanda Mossor, 17

In Love, What I've Become

Wow, yesterday he smiled at me! That's never happened before.
Or maybe he was laughing at the sweatshirt that I wore.

I can't believe I change my clothes a hundred times a day,
And when I think I've found what's right, I still run the other way.

I think up all those witty things that I intend to say.
Then when he comes up to me, I just blush and walk away.

That seems to be the easy part, this zombie who can't speak.
I fall apart when he comes near, and my knees get weak!

Who is this weirdo person I've suddenly become?
Each day I have to ask myself why I've grown so dumb.

Why can't I just go up to him and tell him how I feel?
Instead, I simply tell my friends; it's bizarre and so unreal.

I've made a list of all the things that won't work when he's around!

Can't talk, can't walk, and what's with those goofy sounds?

Now I'm bumping into things; I stutter when I speak.

I sometimes use too much perfume, surely I must reek!

My smile is no longer good enough, and I really hate my hair.

My eyes! My ears! My nose—all wrong; my shape is like a pear!

My clothes: completely out of style. My makeup: really drab.

My laughter: all but disappeared. My shoes: they need rehab.

My heart is but an empty shell and aches throughout the night.

My stomach churns, my heart deflates, my pulse rate isn't right.

Teachers don't understand—once sweet, now Grinch instead.

My parents just gave up on me. My pet does not get fed.

It's all because of this one boy my life is such a mess,

A boy I cannot hold or touch, can't kiss and can't caress!

I know that I should tell him, and let him understand,

My love for him is very real, but his interest seems so bland.

I know I can't go on this way—I'm not even on his "list."

Why has fate bestowed on me a plot with such a twist?

How come it is he doesn't see the sorry state that I am in,

And want to make it up to me, to see my suffering end?

Just how long can he ignore the way my heart does yearn?

Or maybe fate has chosen him, for me to live and learn.

There must be many lessons here on which I have to work,

And then one day I'll understand, why he (or is it me) is such a jerk.

—**Alynn Kirk, 16**

Anatomy of First Love: Nine Kisses

I was sitting in the school cafeteria having lunch with my friends, Amanda and Rachel, when a really cute boy, who I'd never seen before, walked by.

"Amanda!" he called out, just to get her attention. We all looked up and Amanda waved at him, and then, as though he was no big deal, she turned her attention back to the discussion the three of us were having.

"Wow!" I whispered so that only Amanda and Rachel could hear. "He's so cute. Who is he?"

"Paul Turkell," Amanda said, "ninth-grader."

Our school is in the shape of the letter H, as in Herbert Hoover, the thirty-fourth president. Grades six to nine attend classes at our school and each grade has classes in a different part of the H. So we hardly ever run into kids in other grades. Even though the cafeteria is in the center of the building and everyone eats in the same place, for the most part we all go to lunch at different times, so we usually don't run into students in different grades there either. That's probably why I hadn't noticed Paul Turkell. He was a "freshman," and I was only in the seventh grade.

It was already April 15th, and for the rest of the school year, I saw freshman Paul Turkell only six more times: April 24th, 26th, May 7th, 16th, 26th and June 2nd (which was also the last day of school). On those times, Paul and I would wave to each other. That's as far as our friendship went until summer vacation, when we ran into each other four times in Walgreen's. Each time we did, we were both with our mothers, but we would stand together and talk about school stuff until our mothers were ready to leave the store. Towards the end of the summer, we traded phone numbers. That's when we began calling each other. I had never had a boy as a friend before, and it was fun.

When the next school year began, Paul James Turkell was now a sophomore and went to the high school, which was in a different part of town. So, for the first three months of school, I never saw him. But almost every day we would text or call one another. We'd chat about our day and other general things—like when his dog had to spend the night at the animal hospital because he had eaten through an electrical wire while digging in the yard, or the huge scene at my house when my nineteen-year-old sister got her nose pierced.

Then we started sharing some of our most sacred secrets with each other—like how much he liked a certain girl at school (even if she didn't like him) and how much I was looking forward to having a boyfriend. We even talked about how many kids we'd each like to have when we grew up and got married. At the start of the second nine-week school term, we discovered we both love to sing, and dance. So we decided to audition at our local community playhouse for *Grease*, a production that was advertising for teens who could sing and dance to star in its upcoming season of plays. This meant Paul and I would have to practice dance routines together. So for two weeks we met at the community playhouse where the staff of the production had set aside a practice room for those intending to try out for the production.

The more Paul and I practiced, the more I started having feelings for him—as a boyfriend. But I wasn't too sure if I should tell him because I knew he liked Natalie Parker, a girl in his class at school. Then one afternoon when Paul and I were at a rehearsal, he said: "I like you."

I was completely shocked. Now I really wanted him for a boyfriend. So I told him I liked him too.

"I know," he said, smiling.

So my first guy friend became my first boyfriend. I was on top of the world. I went to school the next day in the best mood ever. Things got even better when, just two days later, Paul called me and asked me to the sophomore semi-formal, telling me he wanted me to dance with only him.

I was really sure he would be the only guy with whom I even wanted to dance.

For the rest of my entire life.

Throughout all of human history.

Forever.

And ever.

I did only dance with him. And it was incredible, another "something" I had never experienced. Then on our third dance, Paul pulled me close and sang the entire song to me. It was awesome, and right then and there I knew for sure I was totally in love with him. And I was sure he must feel the same way, because he and I danced to every single song at the dance. During the very last song, "End of the Road," I looked into his eyes and told him I'd love him forever. As we sadly said good night, he kissed my cheek and gave me a hug.

Six days later, Paul asked me to go with him after school to pick up his paycheck at a place he works part-time. The entire way there and back, we held hands. And when he dropped me off at my house, he rubbed his cheek across my forehead, and then kissed my forehead a total of nine times.

Nine times!

My friends, Amanda and Rachel, have both been kissed. Rachel twice by Ben Henry. Amanda's had a lot of kisses, too—six—once by Raymond

Lux, once by Clay Lloyd, and four times by Joey Edwards. But I've been kissed nine times. Nine! And all nine by Paul James Turkell, my true love!

Then, just two weeks later, the day after my birthday to be exact, Paul said he thought we should be "just friends." That was it. Just like that. Not my boyfriend, just back to being my "friend."

Then, two weeks and one day later, I was at a party at his friend's place and Paul was there with a girl from school, Krissy. The two of them started kissing. I started crying. When Paul saw me crying, he came over and asked what was wrong.

"It's hard to be *just friends*," I told him.

"I know," he said. "I miss you, too. So, let's be friends so we can talk about things."

I thought about how good it felt to talk with him and decided that having Paul as a friend was better than not being able to talk with him. I know he'll never be my boyfriend again because he told me he should be with girls who are at least as old as he is. So, that's that. But I will always remember how he was my first boyfriend, and all the things I felt because of him.

Especially those nine kisses.

For a first boyfriend, I think that's a good record!

—Nicole Syngajewski, 15

How Far I'll Go

How far will I go? Pretty far, when it comes to Sheree.

I asked Sheree to the school dance. She insisted I wear a tux, even though it was black-tie optional. I rented a tux to please her, even though I prefer clothes that are more casual and comfortable.
How far will I go? Pretty far, when it comes to Sheree.

Sheree insisted on arriving at the dance in a limo! I really couldn't afford it, but nevertheless, I worked the extra hours on my part-time job—even though it was finals and I needed the time to study.
How far will I go? Pretty far, when it comes to Sheree.

It was time to sign up for the next semester's schedule. I'd planned to take a third year of Spanish to complete my college entry requirements for a foreign language. But Sheree wanted me to take French with her. "It's so much more romantic," she said. I took French for the sole reason of being in the same class with Sheree.
How far will I go? Pretty far, when it comes to Sheree.

"Let's double-date with my best friend Tom,"

I suggested. "Let's not," she said. "He's a nerd, and besides, I don't like the girl he dates." Sheree had a different circle of friends, so I went places with Sheree and her friends, and I didn't seem to see much of my friends anymore. When it came to going out with friends, we just always seemed to end up with hers.

How far will I go? Pretty far when it comes to Sheree.

Sheree called and said that if I didn't take her to the library, she'd get an F in tomorrow's assignment. I told Sheree I'd made a promise to my father that I'd never take the car without his permission. Despite the fact that I couldn't reach my father until later that evening—and because Sheree was so insistent—I took Sheree to the library.

How far will I go? Six weeks all totaled—that's how far I would go with Sheree! Six weeks into the relationship, I started the new semester with a lie between me and my father, not having seen much of my friends, and a class I didn't need—and without one I did.

How far will I go?

Well, pretty far now that I'm not with Sheree. I've learned not to give up the things that are really important to me, the things I value and that make me happy, and move me toward my goals, keeping the promises I make with important people, like friends and my parents.

But that doesn't mean I've signed off on love—I just learned not to ever go that far again.
                              —Christopher Gillian, 17

The "Side Effects" of Love

I'm in love, and it sure brings out the best in me! Just ask anyone who knows me! Now that I have a boyfriend, I'm so much more together. Love is very motivating.

"Are you making the honor roll this quarter?" I asked Kyle Wilson one day in the cafeteria, just to strike up a conversation.

"Sure, aren't you?" he replied.

"Hope so," I said, knowing there was probably a better chance of me winning the lottery—and I'm too young to play. But hearing the expectation in his voice that I would be on the honor roll with him, I was determined that "yes" I would be on the honor roll—even if I'd only made it one other time in the last two years. Then, in the next breath, Kyle asked me if I'd like for him to "swing by my house" to go to the library with him later that evening.

From that very "first date," I've taken every single one of my books home, because I decided then and there, I was going to study harder than ever! I mean, since Kyle really cares about getting good grades, and his goal is to be on the honor roll (and his last girlfriend was Debbie Corso, the smartest girl in our class), it made me think about my own grades. When I started going out with him, my grades were just average. I did what I needed to do to get by. But knowing good grades are important to him, now I work harder on keeping my own grades up.

I've even enlisted my good friends Melinda and Morgan. We always get together after school, just to hang out. We listen to music, talk, laugh and just mess around, but we didn't do homework. Until now! It's made our grades better, and our friendship too.

"Where do you keep the vacuum bags, Mom?" I asked one Saturday last month.

"Why do you want to know?" my mother questioned, looking honestly puzzled. Well, she almost fell over when I said I wanted to vacuum the carpets.

"Kyle is picking me up, so I think I'll vacuum," I told her. My mother walked around looking like she was the one who had won the lottery. Making her that happy actually felt good. Now, I'm in the habit of doing my part to help keep the house picked up and neat.

Having Kyle in my life has some good "side effects." For example, now that I'm getting my homework done each weekday, rather than procrastinating and letting it go until the weekend, I can spend time with Kyle on the weekends. Since my homework is done on time, my parents don't have to constantly remind me to get on it, which means we're all in a better mood.

It's really cool how once I started acting more responsible, my parents started to give me more respect. All these things that they used to have to nag me about, I now find myself doing because of

Kyle. He just brings out the best in me. Not only does it make all my relationships better, but I'm real sure I'll be on the honor roll next quarter. About that time, I may even be wearing Kyle's class ring!

Like I said, love is very motivating!

—Erin Conley, 17

Why Boys Argue with You

Joel and I had been going together for one week when we got into our first argument. I have no idea what we disagreed about, but I do remember everything about the fight. It happened when we were sitting together at a basketball game for my school. Joel just got up and walked out of the gym. Like I said, I don't remember what was said, or why he left, but he did.

After he left, I sat there, not knowing what to do. At first I was just confused over what happened, but the next moment my heart ached at the thought of being on the outs with him. I wanted to tell him that I was so sorry, that I didn't mean whatever it was I did, or whatever it was I said. So, I ran after him to tell him.

He kept walking away. I caught up with him, and wrapped my arm around his waist and told him I was sorry. Chasing after him, he pretended I wasn't there, too cool to notice that I was even living on the same planet, much less had my arms wrapped around him.

So I let go and let him walk away. Besides, I didn't know what to do or say to him to get him to stop pouting. I slowly walked back into the gym not wanting to talk to anyone, stared at the floor, pulling my hair into my face to hide the tears trailing down my face. I made my way back to the spot where he and I had been sitting hoping our "fight" hadn't been too noticeable to others. Eventually, Joel came back and stood with his friends, not far away from where we had been sitting. I felt like running over and giving him a big hug to tell him I loved him and how sorry I was. But I just stayed in my seat and glanced at him. I really didn't know what else to do.

Then walked over and sat down next to me, grabbed my hand and just held it. We didn't say anything for a while, then he said, "I'm sorry. It was all my fault."

I said, "No, I'm sorry. It was my fault—a misunderstanding."

That was our first argument, our first fight. It was also the night of our first kiss.

Joel and I have been liking each other for more than four months now and we've had many arguments. As I've gotten to know Joel better, I've decided I really don't know much about love, or boys.

At least now I've learned what to say when we're having an argument: the truth.

Sometimes the truth calls for an apology, but then again, sometimes the truth means not taking the blame for something that isn't of my doing. And I no longer run after Joel when he gets up and walks away.

I no longer assume his behavior is about something I've done or said. Now that our relationship isn't brand new, I'm learning to be secure enough to not feel like I have to do that anymore.

Just a few days ago Joel told me, "We may fight a lot, but we sure make up beautifully." I have to agree with him on both points.

Maybe that's why boys argue; they like the feelings of drama, and making up.

Or, at least that's what I've learned about love, so far.

—Melissa Hamil, 15

Always, Someone Is Happy

My friends Trevor and Samantha were in love.

Then they broke up.

Now Trevor and Leanna are in love, and Cody and Samantha are in love.

LOVE ...

It comes and goes as it pleases

Never failing to make someone happy.

Pretty cool!

—**Kayleigh Minutella, 13**

What Are You Saying About My "Ex"?

Josh and I broke up after we'd been going together for almost a year. When we talked about not seeing each other anymore, we promised each other we'd always be friends. I found out that's very hard when you first break up. It hurt whenever I saw him. Going from being his girlfriend to just being his friend was a strange feeling—and it wasn't an easy transition.

When I'd see him at school or places the two of us used to hang out, I didn't know how to act around him, especially if he was talking with another girl. Or, if I was with my friends and then discovered he was nearby, I'd pretend not to notice him, yet I'd hope he'd see me.

At school, I'd even walk by some of his classes again and again just so he'd catch a glimpse of me. But if I would find myself in the same hall with him, or in the cafeteria at the same time he was, or when I saw him with his guy friends at the movies or someplace, I'd try not to let him see me. But then after he was gone or out of sight, I'd look around for him, or ask my girlfriends a thousand-and-one questions about where he had gone!

Why does love have to be such carzy-making? I didn't want him to see me, but the moment he was out of sight, I wished he had seen me! I didn't want to talk to him, but I did want to talk to him! It really was a confusing time.

I've also learned something else about love. It can change your perspective on things. For example, as you'd expect, my girlfriends tried to make me feel better and encouraged me to "move on." At first they'd say rotten things about Josh in order to make me feel better. They'd say things like, "He's such a jerk for not wanting to be with you, but don't worry, you will find someone better." Even though they meant well, they were just trying to soothe and comfort me, their comments didn't make me feel better at all. In fact, they did just the opposite. They made feel bad about myself, wondering how I could like someone they thought was such a loser. Their comments didn't take into account that I knew my boyfriend better than they did, even if he is my "ex." He's really a nice person, a genuine good guy.

I didn't like my friends saying that he wasn't. This was a new feeling for me, because before when I'd decided I no longer wanted to like a guy, I'd join in on "trashing" him. But with Josh, it just didn't feel right to do that. I was, after all, once "in love" with him. So one day, after a friend made a derogatory comment about him, I said, "I know you're only saying that to make me feel better, but I'm not going to trash Josh just because we're not dating anymore. Even if we have broken up, he'll always be my friend. Just like you're my friend and I wouldn't go along with anyone talking bad about you."

My friend looked really surprised. "Wow," she

said. "That's cool. I hadn't thought of it that way, but I really do get it."

I don't think your friends expect you to defend an "ex."

I'd say love is a good teacher.

—Helena Longfellow, 16

Alexis + James

Alexis + James
James + Alexis
Alexis Hall & James Bradley
Alexis Anne Hall & James Jeffrey Bradley

James Bradley
James Jeffrey Bradley
James J. Bradley
J. J. Bradley

Alexis Bradley
Alexis Anne Bradley
Alexis A. Bradley
A. H. Bradley

Ms. Alexis Bradley
Mrs. Alexis Bradley
Ms. Alexis Hall-Bradley
Mrs. Alexis Hall-Bradley

Mrs. James Bradley
Mrs. James Jeffrey Bradley
Mr. & Mrs. Bradley
Mr. & Mrs. Hall-Bradley

Alexis loves James
James loves Alexis

—Alexis Hall, 15

Killer Fashion Sense

Dear Love of My Life,

I once thought that I knew what it was to love a girl, but what I felt was a pale comparison to what you inspire in me.

When I think of you, when I see your picture, my breathing actually stops momentarily, arrested under the weight of all my feelings of love and passion.

Words will never be enough to tell you how I feel.

My love is deeper than the sea, higher than the highest cloud, a force greater than thunder, lightning and the mightiest hurricane.

You've become my reason for living—for existing. I would gladly lay everything I own—and everything I will ever own—before your feet if you would only give me but a portion of the love I am willing to give you, an eternal love, I am certain.

When I wake up in the morning, my first thoughts are of your smile, and because I'm filled with anticipation of thinking of you all day, the sun comes out, the skies get blue and flowers bloom.

When I go to sleep at night, visions of you lead me into a world of the sweetest dreams. Knowing that you live and breathe and sleep at that moment, here in the very same universe as I do, gives my life greater meaning, my soul greater purpose. Say that you'll be mine, and let's build those dreams together. If you would agree to be my one and only love, I would commit my entire life, my heart and soul, my very being, to showering you with love and devotion.

I know many others must love you for all the reasons I do—your beauty, your smile, your killer fashion sense—but I am absolutely certain no one will ever love you as much as I do.

When I think of the immeasurable depth of my love for you, I can't believe that I first saw you only three short months ago! Yet, I really believe I've known you for an eternity.

I know we are destined to be together, because we are soul mates, who have always been together in a realm outside of time. With that first look at your picture in my sister's Seventeen magazine, I just knew we were fated to be together.

You've yet to meet me, and I realize I don't have a great career like you do as a model, but I do have great potential. I get good grades, know my way around the Web and plan to go to college. More importantly, I would bring you more happiness than anyone else in the world could ever hope to.

I can only ask with all sincerity, will you please go out with me?

All My Love, I Give to You Forever,
Peter

P. S. Seventeen magazine has returned my letter, so I sent it in to be published in this book, hoping you would read it. When you do, you can write me care of the authors.

I'll be waiting!

—Peter Colucci, 15

Richard, Richard on My Mind

Richard, Richard on my mind,
I think about you *all* the time.
I dream of you every single night,
Thoughts of you flood my days with light.

Every day my heart grows fonder,
Even so, I have to wonder,
Is this true, is this real?
I can't control the way I feel.

I'd love to hold you oh so near,
And softly whisper in your ear.
Can we hug? Or take a walk?
Go on a date? Or just go talk?

Can I kiss you? Can I call?
Say yes, I'll give my all.
The pain I feel when we're apart
I'll tell you now, it breaks my heart!

Richard, Richard on my mind,
I think about you all the time.
I dream of you every single night,
I LOVE YOU, so love me, too, all right?
—Thelma Wright, 14

Absolutely P-r-o-m-i-s-e-d

Dear Grant,

Just so you know, I'm never speaking to you again! I can't believe that you could stand me up after you promised—absolutely promised—that you would meet me in the library after school. I'm through—and I mean through!!! I warned you yesterday when you didn't meet me outside my last-period class to walk me to the bus, and now this! Both times you said you'd be there, but you weren't. You promised—p-r-o-m-i-s-e-d—you'd be there! I don't even know how you can live with yourself!

Obviously, your word, your promises, mean absolutely nothing to you. So they mean absolutely nothing to me from here on out. Just like you mean absolutely nothing to me from here on out. I am not the kind of girl who can be taken for granted. You'll see; I'm not going to speak to you ever again. Don't even bother trying to speak to me. I don't even want you looking at me. You just live your life and I'll live mine, because we are definitely over. Our relationship is a thing of the past. Just pretend I'm invisible, and I'll pretend you are invisible. Just pretend we are on different planets—obviously you're from a different planet. That ought to make it easy enough not to speak to me, because I am never going to speak to you again. Ever!

I'm beyond apologies, so don't even try. No

excuse or apology could be good enough to explain away your standing me up yesterday and now again, today! Just so there's no doubt, I'll say it again: I'm never going to speak to you again. Don't think I'm not serious, because I've never been more serious.

Once Yours, Now Forever Silent,
Heather

P. S. If you want to talk about any of this, you can meet me after sixth period or call me after school today. And if you would like to start our breakup after Saturday night, that would be okay with me, too—since there is the dance and you know they'll play our favorite song. It would probably also be good for us to have just one more kiss. You owe me.

—Heather Solice, 15

My Hands They Quiver, My Feet They Quake...

Last year I wrote a poem for Aaron, a boy in my class. I had a huge crush on him. I found the letter the other day and was so happy and relieved I hadn't given it to him! I'd be so embarrassed! Thank goodness I never got up the nerve to actually give him the poem. Here it is:

When I See You

When I see you my heart it thumps,
My body is covered with little goose bumps,
My hands they quiver, my feet they quake,
And I feel like I'm a chocolate milkshake.
You may not believe I can love you this true,
But that's how I feel when I see you.

I can't believe I was actually going to send this to Aaron! One of the nice things about growing up is you can see just how silly some of the things you did when you were younger really were. Giving the poem to Aaron would have been a very stupid thing to do. I mean, you can't waste a good love poem on a short-lived romance, and I don't like Aaron anymore. But I am a proud survivor of heartbreak, and this year I like his best friend Tommy Moran.

I'm sure glad I didn't waste my masterpiece on

Aaron, because I'm planning on giving it to Tommy instead!

What I've learned is love can come and go, so you have to be really careful about sending out your best romantic notes. (Or, you might want to make a copy so you can use it again when you fall in love with somebody else.) Good inspiration is a terrible thing to waste.

—Kristi Powers, 14

You've Gone and Left Me Lonely

Dear Jean,

It seems you've gone and left me lonely,
So I write this plea for your heart only,
Please remember all that was once ours
And accept the message of these flowers.

Red and yellow roses for the words so hard to find:
Red for the passion and the tender ties that bind,
Yellow as an offering to right all the things gone
wrong;
As a symbol of apology, assuring my remorse is
strong.

The thorn on every stem, a pain in my heart,
As every cruel word I spoke now pierces me apart.
The sweet scent of the blossoms speaks of all the
fun we had,
And begs a chance to restore that good and to erase
the bad.

Take my bouquet with my words sincere,
The feelings they express are real and clear,
Forgive me please and let me prove to you,
My love is real, and will be forever true.

—Phil Salley, 18

Will You Marry Me?

Dear Danny,

You,
The Love of my life,
With a smile on your face,
Asked, "Will you marry me?"

My answer:

YES YES YES YES YES YES YES YES YES
YES YES YES YES YES YES YES YES YES YES
YES YES YES YES YES YES YES YES YES YES
YES YES YES YES YES YES YES YES YES YES
YES YES YES YES YES YES YES YES YES YES
YES YES YES YES YES YES YES YES YES YES
YES YES YES YES YES YES YES YES YES YES
YES YES YES YES YES YES YES YES YES YES
YES YES YES YES YES YES YES YES YES YES
YES YES YES YES YES YES YES YES YES YES
YES YES YES YES YES YES YES YES YES YES
YES YES YES YES YES YES YES YES YES YES
YES YES YES YES YES YES YES YES YES YES
YES YES YES YES YES YES YES YES YES YES
YES YES YES YES YES YES YES YES YES YES
YES YES YES YES YES YES YES YES YES YES
YES YES YES YES YES YES YES YES YES YES
YES YES YES YES YES YES YES YES YES YES

YES YES YES YES YES YES YES YES YES YES
YES YES YES YES YES YES YES YES YES YES
YES YES YES YES YES YES YES YES YES YES
YES YES YES YES YES YES YES YES YES YES
YES YES YES YES YES YES YES YES YES YES
YES YES YES YES YES YES YES YES YES YES
YES YES YES YES YES YES YES YES YES YES
YES YES.

—Daniella Wells, 15

Holes in the Sky

Last summer my mother's family had a reunion. All of my cousins and second cousins were there. The teenagers all hung out with me; they were really cool. We listened to CDs and talked and laughed and had a really good time.

There were also about a billion old people there—and all of them were related to me, too! What I noticed about these "old geezers" (as we kids secretly called them) was how different they all were. There were some who sat around and didn't look much interested in each other or much of anything—and especially didn't look interested in us younger kids. Some of them commented on the way some of the teens dressed and wore our hair, and they weren't very nice comments. It was obvious they considered it their role to "tolerate" us, but probably only because the day would be over and they wouldn't be seeing us until a year or more later. You just knew they didn't really accept us, or even necessarily like us. I'm not trying to put them down; it's just you could tell they hated the music we played. They even complained about the state of the world—as if our music created it.

Then there were some of the older set who smiled and seemed interested in us. You could see they came to the reunion with the intention of being open to the things that were going on, and to everyone who had come. I appreciated how nice they were.

Then there was old Aunt Lottie (who is really my great-aunt)! She has to be about eighty years old. "Great song," she commented once, smiling real big and shaking her head to the music. "I love music that can put holes in the sky!" I thought that was a cool comment. "Don't you ever forget how to love music and dancing," she commented. "It's the wind that sets love to spinning the world around!" I think that is a perfectly hip thing to say.

I knew right then and there that I want to stay forever young at heart just like my Great-Aunt Lottie. I hope I'm as full of life and fun as she is, and not old and grouchy like some old people.

I'm starting to think "young" now, because I think grouchy old people are grouchy young people, and people who are full of life and fun when they are old were full of life and fun when they were young, too.

My hope is to be forever young at heart—like Great-Aunt Lottie.

—Lerissa Dennison, 15

"Dr. Santos"

When I was seven years old, I got spinal meningitis and was really sick in the hospital. While I was there, the doctor not only saved my life, he was also really good to me. Every day, he took the time to make me smile and was always friendly. He never treated me like I was too young to understand what it meant to have spinal meningitis and what he planned to do to treat it. He also didn't think I was too young to have an opinion about my treatment. That made me feel like a real part of the team, and I'm sure it was important to my getting well.

It also was a big factor in my decision to become a doctor when I got better and finished school. I knew I wanted to be just like him. Then for a long time, I forgot all about it, until I was in high school and it was time to decide what classes I needed to get into a college. This forced me to think about what I was going to do with my life. I knew I wanted a career where I could really make a difference in the world, one where I knew I was doing something that would help other people—and I recalled the doctor who healed me, and decided practicing medicine would be a wonderful way to use my life. So I renewed my desire to be a doctor.

I believe it's good to visualize myself doing what I hope for most in life, so now I picture myself in a white coat with a stethoscope hanging around my neck, my diploma on the wall, and being able to help and heal others. Remembering my doctor, his kindness as well as how he healed me by being a great physician, gives me a perfect role model for moving toward my goal. My excitement for being a doctor is at an all-time high. I'm in my first year of college working toward that goal.

Being a doctor and healing others is what I hope for most in life; it's my first love.

—**Craig Santos, 19**

Keeping Tabs on John

A memory of a loving moment is forever: Though a certain guy is no longer in my life, I can still feel him removing my glasses and kissing me.
        —Tracey Seiple, 16

Secretly, I had a huge crush on John Joseph, and for nearly a whole year, I'd been keeping tabs on him. There were a couple of big hurdles to our getting together, however. The first was that he didn't know I existed. Still, the biggest hurdle was that we're in different circles at school. John is a jock. I'm a "band-o"—a band geek.

At my school jocks date ONLY cheerleaders. They're expected to. A popular jock dating a band geek would be out of the question. My heart and I watched John Joseph, from a distance, week in and week out.

Finally, one day my heart asked me, "What's to lose if we talked to him?"

Given that it was already October, I thought it was a fair question. My next step was to find a way to be in the same place he was, like maybe the library, and then go up to him and start talking. How was John J. ever going to know that I was alive and sharing the same earth as he if somebody didn't let him know?

That one day arrived.

I was entering the library, where I planned to return Flowers for Algernon. John was walking into the library at the same time! Spotting the book, I was holding, he asked, "Are you returning that?"

"Yes," I replied. "I had to read it for creative writing."

"Oh, you must be taking Mrs. Wilson's class, too," he said. "Have you already done the paper on it? I haven't started. Well, that figures, because I haven't even read the book! In fact, I've not even checked out the book."

And that's when I said as coolly as I could, "Well, it's a great book but slow reading. It'll take you all of two days for sure."

"Really," he groaned. "I don't have two days. I've got an out-of-town game after school tomorrow, so Coach said it was going to be a long and late practice tonight." Then he looked at me and asked, "Where do you live? Are you pretty close, because maybe you could tell me the whole story and I could sort of write my paper from your executive summary!" With this he laughed, and I realized the crush of my life just asked me to get together with him!

"I don't live too far from school," I answered, trying to think of what to say next, as a million and one questions went through my head: "Would Mom and Dad care if I had a boy over after dinner? Would Mom ban my little brother to his room so that he wouldn't pester us and so that I'd have private time with John? Was the house clean enough to have him over? Would he want snacks—what snacks? Would popcorn be okay, or would chips be better? What kind of chips—jalapeño, or just plain ones? No onions for sure. Dip? Would it be good to have dip with the chips? Should I suggest he come over right after his football practice, or ask him to come over after he's done with dinner? If I put it off that long, might John call and suggest I just tell him the story over the phone? What if . . .?"

"Give me your address and I'll stop over right after practice," he said, interrupting my stress attack.

"Okay. Sure," I said, trying to sound as cool as I could under the circumstance. I gave him my address, phone number and cell number, and an alternative phone number in case he couldn't reach me on any of the others.

It was nearly six o'clock when he arrived—with a six-pack of sodas and a bag of chips in hand! I took him to the television room, shut the door and began telling him the story and reading him certain parts that I'd found interesting. Every now and then John would ask a question. A couple of times he asked me to reread a certain paragraph. I could tell that he was really getting into the book. He especially had taken Charlie, the book's central character, to heart.

I had taken John Joseph to heart!

Because of the out-of-town game, John didn't come the following evening, but he did the night after that. I was just nearing the end of the book, where Gimpy is telling Charlie about the importance of friends, ". . . we want you to remember that you've got friends here . . . it's good to have friends. . . ," I read.

"It's good to have you," John said tenderly. Then, he took my glasses off and kissed me on the forehead.

I fell in love right then and there of course.

"Want to go for a walk?" he asked. "Would your parents will mind?"

"Be right back, Mom!" I yelled, heading out the door with this gorgeous guy. Did I care that I didn't get my algebra done? Not in the least! We walked around the block in my neighborhood and then he left. I was in seventh heaven.

Unfortunately, as easy as the two days came, they passed without any more interaction between us. A couple of days later John was named our school's "Mr. Football"—our school's male equivalent to being voted homecoming queen. Homecoming was less than a week away, and as expected, John asked Tara Wells, a cheerleader.

Three months have passed, and John is still dating Tara. But sometimes I'll look over in his direction and catch him glancing over in my direction. When that happens, I can just feel that kiss all over again.

What I've discovered is that even a memory of a loving moment is forever: Whenever I look at him,

I can still feel him removing my glasses and kissing me.

It is so romantic—still. I'm not going to ever give up hope that one day he will do that again.

—Tracey Seiple, 16

Your Boyfriend...Ought to be Mine!

Some guys make better boyfriends than do others.

—Daniella Chopra, 15

Ty Wilkins has green eyes, brown hair and the best smile in the whole world. From the moment I saw this guy, my heart dumped—for good, this time—my old boyfriend! I had never been so attracted to a guy before! But here's the problem: Ty is the boyfriend of my best friend, Samantha Milner—who just happens to also be my cousin—and we go to the same school!

I didn't plan on falling in love with my cousin's boyfriend.

What happened is that Sammy and I had made plans to go to the state fair together. At the very last minute she asked Ty (her boyfriend) to come along. They'd been a couple for about three months. Though I'd never met him, from everything she'd told me about him, I figured the two of them were seeing only one another. Some guys make better boyfriends than do others, and Sammy had described Ty as a cool guy. He sent her texts all the time. He sat with her at lunch without being bashful like some guys are. And when there was a school dance, he bought the tickets. Stuff like that. Ty certainly sounded to me like a good boyfriend! I thought she was a lucky girl to have a boyfriend who really, really liked her.

So that's why I was so surprised that when the three of us met up at the entrance of the fair, there was an immediate attraction between Ty and me. Trying to calm down my fluttering heart, the moment we started walking I looked around to see if there was a stand where we could get some food. "Yum! Hamburgers on the grill," I said excitedly as we passed by one of the food stands. The moment I said that, I remembered that Sammy is a full-fledged vegetarian, strongly for PETA, and here I was, suggesting we eat meat! Immediately, Ty spoke up saying, "Awesome! They have elk burgers, too." I looked at Ty and he was grinning. We looked at each other, and as though we could read each other's mind, headed for that food stand.

Then Ty and I were ordering while Sammy chastised us for eating meat. As though he couldn't care less, he said, "Two huge hamburgers, please." Then, while eating—Sammy, having French fries only—Ty chomps at the burger and says, "Oh man, nothing like a hamburger!" Personally, I thought his teasing her in that way was probably unnecessary, but I took it as flirting with her and just laughed along with him. As the three of us sat at the food stand, Ty commented that once, while on a trip to Florida with his parents, he'd tasted alligator meat. Well, I had a very similar experience when I'd been on a school trip and we'd visited an alligator farm. After the tour, we ate in the cafeteria, and it just so happened that alligator meat was on the menu.

I ordered it. That both Ty and I had tried alligator meat seemed an interesting coincidence. "Alligator is really good," I said.

"It is. It's great. Better than chicken," Ty remarked. Sammy scrunched up her face and groaned, "Oh, gross!"

As we continued to talk, I discovered that Ty and I had a lot in common: We each had one brother and two sisters, and both of us were the oldest. We liked the same music; we both preferred casual to dress up; and we both had the same kind of pet—a snake! We both played soccer and we're both Lutherans. That we were both so much alike was just incredible. We could have talked for hours. I'm not saying that Ty ignored Sammy. He was very affectionate toward her, and she toward him. Like when we would enter exhibits, he'd open the door for her or always ask if she wanted a Coke or ice cream or anything. Still, it seemed to me like they were mismatched. I mean, they didn't really talk between themselves.

We stayed at the fair for most of the afternoon and then left for home. On the way to Sammy's house I commented that my back was hurting because I had done a flip on the trampoline in gym class and done it wrong. "I'll give you a back rub when we get to Sammy's house," Ty offered. And he did.

Pretty soon I had to get home, and Ty offered to take me home. Samantha came along, of course.

When we got to my house, I gave Samantha a hug and said good-bye to Ty. He gave me a quick hug, saying, "That was fun. Call me if you need to talk or anything." Turning again to say good-bye to Samantha, I then saw the look of hurt in her eyes. It was clear that she understood that Ty had feelings for me. It had to be an awful day for her!

I called Samantha later that evening and apologized for talking so much to Ty.

"Promise me you won't call him," she said. I gave her my word that I wouldn't, so I won't.

Two weeks have passed, and so far I've kept my word. But I've still got strong feelings for Ty. I'm hoping that Samantha and Ty break up. Still, I've decided that until the two of them break up, I'll just be patient. I do think it's just a matter of time until they do. But like I said, my heart also feels for Samantha knowing Ty and I "clicked" as we did.

But a promise is a promise, and I'm not going to hurt my friend by "stealing" her boyfriend. I had that happen to me once, and I learned that to be betrayed by a best friend hurts more than does having someone leave you for another.

I'll wait for Ty to come to me.

It's just a matter of waiting on love.

—Daniella Chopra, 15

"We've Got to Talk ... NOW!"

Here's the thing about love: It makes you a bit crazy.. Whether you've just fallen in love—or you've just been dumped—either way, you do and say some silly, and sometimes stupid, things.
—Lindsey Rubia, 16

What was so important that my boyfriend of four months had given my best friend a note telling me to meet him "Right now, because we've got to talk"? I asked the teacher for a restroom pass and headed for the back hall where we always met up. As I watched my boyfriend approach me—looking his usual cool—I looked to see if he'd turn on his "puppy dog" look, something he always did when he saw me.

He didn't.

As hard as I tried not to feel insecure, I was. Was Dylan delivering good news, or not? We'd been a couple for four months, though the last few weeks hadn't gone so well. There had been the fight over Monica Green, which was her own fault because she had started a rumor that Dylan was breaking up with me. And Dylan and I had fought over his not calling three nights ago, as he'd promised. He'd been especially quiet the last two days. And just yesterday he stood me up rather than walking me to class. But most disturbing was that when I called his house last night, his mom said he couldn't come to the phone. That wasn't a good sign.

Trying to get a quick read on things, I noticed that Dylan was walking fast—and not smiling. What was he upset about? I tried to think positive. I smiled. I tried not to look as nervous as I was. "Hi, honey!" I offered, reaching for his hand. He did not offer his. "Lindsey," he said, not saying hello or asking how I was, "You've got to stop calling my house and stop writing me notes."

"But we always do," I said in self-defense.

"I know, but not again," he countered. "Things are over between you and me."

"What?" I asked, stunned and then stammered, "Why?" "Because I have feelings for someone else."

Like that. Just like that. That's how things ended between us. He said he was sure things between us couldn't be "worked out." Well that made sense: He had "FEELINGS FOR SOMEONE ELSE"!

I was stunned. Blindsided is more like it. Surely this couldn't be happening. I looked into his eyes and knew he meant it. Four days ago—in the back row at the movies—he'd held my hand, played with my hair and kissed my neck. But that was four days ago! Can four days change things this fast? I demanded an explanation, of course! Impatient, and sensing a "scene," he told me to "relax" and that we could "still be friends." Friends? Friends? After four entire months of being boyfriend and girlfriend we were now going to be "friends"? Who tells these guys to say such stupid things? By now I was sobbing. But Dylan stood there as if the sun was shining. How could he? I was in tears, my heart ripped out. All our plans evaporated. What about our plans for the dance on Friday and the prom in the spring? We'd planned everything out, from how the color of the ribbon on his boutonniere would match the ribbon on my wrist corsage, to which couples we would ask to help share the expense of a limo.

What about all those plans—were they going to be "just friends," too? Can love be canceled so fast? How could all we had thought was so special about the two of us now be special only to me?

"Can I have my jacket back, please?" he asked. I was worried about our lives, and he was worried about his jacket? I was wearing it, so I ripped it off and as hard as I could I threw it at his feet. "Just take your bleeping jacket and get lost!" I screamed, stomping on his jacket.

"That's it! It's really, really over!" he said, making a point of using my being out of control as a reason his decision to leave was a good one. Calmly, obviously feeling vindicated, Dylan picked up his jacket, brushed it off and off he went. Into the sunset. I stood there. Feeling discarded. Devastated. Worse, I'd returned his letter jacket, and he'd probably give it to the new girl to wear.

That was a month ago. I'm better now. My heart doesn't hurt as much as it did in the first days and weeks. And I don't feel so panicky when I sometimes see Dylan in the halls—though I admit that it helps that the new girlfriend has already dumped him!

Now she's the girlfriend of Dylan's best friend—which makes me feel even better.

I think about all this—how love comes and goes. I find it amazing that the heart feels so blessed when loves comes, and so devastated when it leaves. But here's the thing: It'll feel the same the next time around.

And here's something else I've discovered: There's no way around your feelings. You're going to have them. Whether you've just fallen in love or you've just been dumped, either way, you're going to do and say some silly, and sometimes stupid, things. You won't get to decide how you feel; only your heart knows. All you can do is trust yourself to not get too bent out of shape about things. So that's where I'm at for now with the love thing. Hoping that each time when love comes—or goes (and knowing it will), I won't act too weird or crazy.

—Lindsey Rubia, 16

Do You Love Me: Yes or No?

I love being in love! It's so much drama sometimes.

—Dana Giordano, 16

I love being in love! It's so much drama sometimes. There are good times. And sometimes you must prepare for a few days of tears. Not that I have everything figured out. But I'm learning a lot.

My first lesson in love was in the eighth grade. In English class, Billy Thornton passed me a note that read, "Do you like me? Circle 'yes' or 'no.'" Well, I didn't really know for sure. I'd never had a boyfriend. And I hadn't thought about Billy Thornton as a candidate to be my first one. But two of my friends had already had boyfriends, so I circled "yes," walked to the front of the room to sharpen my pencil and on the way past Billy's desk, dropped the note on his desk. That was how I came to have my first boyfriend.

Our being boyfriend and girlfriend was mostly a secret, though. From across the rows of desks in Mrs. Walton's class, Billy would clear his throat to get my attention. Then, with his eyes darting to and fro, he'd alert me to the fact that he had written me a note. It was my job to retrieve the note, which also meant that I had the sharpest pencils in class! Always, these notes were about what a "doad" the teacher was. But what else does one write about in eighth grade? That being my first experience with love, I thought it was romantic. One day Mrs. Walton caught on to our little game and confiscated a note. So that was the last of our romance, one that had lasted all of eleven school days.

For my next boyfriend, I moved on to Brandon Wilkerson. Brandon was my first kiss, my first dance and my first holding hands sort of love. We had three classes together, which meant we could walk to class together and sit together in class if we were working on a group project. We even went to a dance, to a school play and to a baseball game together. It was great fun. Brandon was my sun, my moon and stars. Still, he frustrated me so much. He was argumentative and sometimes he would yell at me for no reason. That seemed like a dumb thing to do with someone who is your girlfriend. After three months of that I had to tell him I needed a better class of boyfriend.

My next experience with love came when I accepted a date to go to a dance with a popular boy, Sid Metzler. For as cute as Sid was, we never really clicked. I think the reason was because my heart still belonged to Billy and Brandon. I was okay with it, though, because I could tell Sid was a little too experienced for me. He thought it was okay to put his hands on my butt when we danced, and that was a little scary to me.

In my next experience, I thought I hit the jackpot.

One morning, standing at my locker with a group of friends, this incredible guy walked over and started talking to my friends. But he kept looking at me, so I knew he was checking me out. His name was Luis Michael Bustillos. He was two grades ahead of me, which is why I'd never seen him up close. We instantly clicked and instantly became an item.

Each morning we would meet up in the student center and just sit and stare into each other's eyes. All day long we'd write each other notes and pass them off to each other. It was so wonderful. Because of him, I learned what "love at first sight" feels like. It's totally wonderful, and I recommend it highly.

But, on the morning of our third week as "an item," he replaced me with a girl in his own class. So that was that. I cried and cried. It was the first time I'd cried over love gone wrong.

Then I decided to give love a rest. Or at least that's the way things turned out. For one full school year I had a real dry spell as far as boys were concerned. Luckily, summer changed my luck.

What happened was, a friend had invited me to her barbecue party. I'd been dancing and decided to get some food. I loaded up my plate, and while looking around for a place to sit, spotted Billy Thornton sitting by the firepit. He was staring at me. He motioned for me to come join him, and I went over and sat next to him. We sat there together for the next full hour—talking about everything under the stars! He asked me if he could drive me home, and since I'd come with friends, I said yes.

Once to my house, we sat in the car and talked for almost another whole hour. If my dad hadn't flipped the porch light on and off several times, we'd probably still be there! Then, the minute Billy got to his house, we talked to each other by e-mail for another half hour. It was so much fun.

That weekend he asked me over to his house to help him wash his car. After that, we watched a corny movie, snuggling on his futon. Right in the middle of the movie, I instinctively kissed him as I turned my head. It was so beautiful, because that kiss told us how each felt about the other.

The next weekend we went to the movies and then we went for a pizza. The next Friday he invited me to watch a concert on television with his family. The weekend after that he came to watch me sing in a choir concert. He'd driven me there, and just before we got out of the car, he reached in the backseat to get the flowers he'd brought me. There were two white roses and a red one. The card read, "Do you love me? 'Yes' or 'no'?"

"Definitely!" I answered. I just love it when a guy steals your heart! Well, that was six months ago. I'm still in love and I expect to feel this way about Billy Thornton for the rest of my life!

—Dana Giordano, 16

That Was Your "Sister"?—Yeah, Right!

I guess I'd classify the kind of love I'm in as the "puppy love" version, because it wore off faster than lip gloss in a kissing contest.

—Tina Convoy, 14

My first experience with love was when I was twelve. His name was Adam Morgan. We weren't really in love, though I thought so at the time. But it was not the kind of love where nothing else in the entire world matters. It was not the kind of love where you can think of nothing all day and night long but that one person. Two of my friends are in love that way, and from talking to them, it sounds like the best kind of love to have. Comparing the kind of love, I was in with Adam Morgan to the kind my friends had, I guess I'd classify mine as the "puppy love" version, because it wore off faster than lip gloss in a kissing contest. Still, I was happy with Adam while it lasted.

The big problem between Adam and me had mostly to do with his splitting his time between his parents. His parents were divorced and living in different towns. His dad lived in my town, but his mom lived twenty miles away. Adam lived with his mom during the week and attended school there, and then spent weekends with his father. I got to see Adam only on the weekends. This meant we were apart all week. He didn't have a computer, so we couldn't e-mail each other during the week. And after racking up a huge long-distance phone bill in the first week we met, neither of our parents would allow us to call the other again.

When we got together on the weekends, it was like we had to start all over again, from nerves to not knowing what to say. Still, I happily considered him my boyfriend.

One Sunday afternoon as we were playing miniature golf, the bomb dropped. We were having a good time, laughing and sharing a Coke from the same can, when Adam told me he loved me. I think he was scared the moment he said these words. I don't think he planned on saying them. I think they just slipped out of his mouth because we were having such a good time. Probably, he should have said, "I like being with you," or something like that. To tell you the truth, "I love you" freaked me out a little, too, because I didn't know what was supposed to happen next.

What did happen was that Adam began to act weird. Like the next weekend we were supposed to hang out at the mall and play games in the arcade. Because he was an hour late, I called his house. A girl answered the phone. "I need to talk to Adam," I said wondering who the girl was. "Adam can't come to the phone," she said and hung up on me. That made me mad, so I called back and demanded, "Put Adam on the phone!"

"Oh, you again," she said, adding, "Don't you

have homework to do or something?" Again, she hung up. I pressed redial and waited for someone to answer. On the three-hundredth ring Adam answered. "Yeah, what?" he asked, obviously irritated. "Who was that girl who answered the phone?" I demanded. "My sister," he said and then sort of laughed. I could hear laughter in the background, so I knew it wasn't just him and his "sister." Then I started to get paranoid because I'm pretty sure Adam does not have a sister. At least he never told me he did. We always talked about his family and he never once mentioned anything about a sister. And you just don't forget to say you've got a sister! I felt strange about things. "You're late! Come pick me up right now!" I demanded.

"Hey, I can't get over there today," he said coolly. "I'll talk to you next weekend." Then he hung up.

I sat there with the phone still to my ear listening to the dial tone for nearly a minute. Then I just bawled. Fifteen minutes later, feeling upset, I called his house again. Once again his "sister" answered. "Tell Adam I'm dumping him," I told her and then hung up. But the moment I hung up, I called right back and blurted, "And tell Adam I think he's a real jerk." I hung up again and cried some more.

I had no way to get to his dad's house or I would have gone over. But since I couldn't get there, I just waited until the next weekend, knowing he'd call. He didn't. I called him. "Have you been cheating on me?" I blurted. "Yeah, sure," he laughed. "I'm going steady with Britney Spears!"

"Yeah, right," I said. "In your dreams!" I hung up knowing I had to dump him for good. So that was the end of my first love, my puppy love. I hurt for a long time over that. What that shows is that even puppy love, when it's over, is a painful thing. Next time, I'm going to skip the puppy love kind and go for something better. I'm new at this, but my friends tell me it doesn't matter if it's your first or last love, because you "Win a few and lose a few, but you have to suit up for them all." I've decided not to be bitter. I'll just take this in stride and when the next love comes along, I'll "suit up" again! One thing is for sure: I'm going to choose someone who doesn't live out of the city, because it's too hard to keep an eye on him! And one of the first things I'm going to ask him is the names and ages of all his sisters.

—Tina Convoy, 14

"I Dare You to Ask Him to Dance..."

If you think you know everything there is to know about love, love will prove you wrong!
                                    —Alaina Ramey, 14

I had just dumped my boyfriend of four months and was feeling lousy. When my friends suggested I go with them to the Valentine's Day Sweetheart Dance at school, I said no. But Christine, Bethy, Tamara, Lindsey, Meredith, Jennifer and Holly talked me into going. So, I did.

Not long after we got there, Bethy dared me to go up to Justin Latta—the most popular boy at school—and ask him to dance with me. "No, way. You're totally crazy!" I told her.

Justin is the coolest guy in the universe, and everyone knows it. Even he knows it! There is no way I was fool enough to do something so stupid! My friends and I pretty much just all stood around and talked about the couples dancing. Some of my friends got asked to dance, and sometimes they just danced with each other, especially if a great tune was played. About a half-hour into the dance, still not one single person had asked me to dance, which I pretty much expected. Practically everyone likes my ex-boyfriend, so it's not like they want to be seen asking his former girlfriend to dance. Besides, some kids didn't even know my boyfriend and I had broken up, so they weren't about to ask me to dance, either. I just knew my being there was a hopeless cause.

But my friends convinced me to stay anyway. Then Lindsey came up with the bright idea that she was going to go around to ask if there was anyone who might like to dance with me. I was mortified and begged her not to. She went anyway. I watched as she made her way through the crowd, asking a zillion boys—all of whom obviously said "no." Then she got to Justin Latta. I thought I would die! Well, soon I see Justin looking in my direction, and I'm thinking he's going to die laughing. But no, he starts walking in my direction. "I didn't know you'd broken up with Seth," he said to me. "I can't say that I'm sorry to hear that! Would you like to dance?"

I thought I was going to faint. I reached out and took his hand, and he led me onto the dance floor. We were the very last couple to leave the dance! We've been dating now for seventeen days. If you think you know everything there is to know about love, love will prove you wrong! I'm betting there isn't one person in the entire universe who can say she knows everything there is to know about love.

—Alaina Ramey, 14

The Grim Reaper

They say you never forget your first love. I'm sure of it.

—**Shire Feingold, 16**

The room was pitch-black. Standing in the dark, I listened as the door creaked open ever so slowly. Then, like a comet, something swooshed into the pitch-black room. All I could hear was the flapping of wings as tiny creatures—like bats or something screeched loudly. Frozen in my tracks, I then heard a blood-curdling scream followed by my little sister's "Little Bo Peep" dress ruffling along the ground. The scream made her scream and then call out, "Oh my Gosh! It's a skeleton!" In the same instant something grabbed my foot. I screamed and jumped back, almost tripping over my floor-length yellow Renaissance dress. Then someone grabbed my arm. It was too strong to be my sister. Terrified, and fighting it off, I strained to see who could possibly be gripping my arm.

This was the most fun haunted house ever!

As the lights came up, I saw all the commotion was caused by the Grim Reaper! And then came the apology: "I am so sorry to have scared you. Are you okay?" At this I started laughing!

His name was Michele. We walked outside, found a seat and started talking. Anything to be together. I could just feel the chemistry between us. We didn't move for the next half hour. We talked about everything from school to our love for music; from writing to sports; and from friends to family. All this time together—and not one awkward moment. It was amazing! Well, there was one disturbance, Little Bo Peep, my little sister kept coming over to me wanting me to take her back into the haunted house. I tried to fend her off, telling her everything from "Little Bo Peep, go find your sheep" to "Bryce, Dad is looking for you" (it was a family-style party). Finally, my dad came to the rescue, and Michele and I were alone again.

Michele had still not removed his mask. I couldn't help wondering what he looked like, and yet I didn't want to ask him to remove it. "What a great buffet," he said. "Let's get some food." We went from table to table, loading up our plates, finally returning to our spot to eat. And that's when Michele reached up to remove his mask. I held my breath, hoping he'd be good looking. He was! Under that mask was the most amazing face! I was mesmerized!

The haunted house was emptying out and Michele asked me if I wanted to talk some more. He said I looked cold, and so he put his arm around me. We walked over to the porch, away from the crowd. As we stood talking, I felt like a princess in a fairy tale: me standing there with my Prince Charming, my long hair and flowing dress just blowing in the wind.

The moon was out. The stars were twinkling. It was just so romantic. Then as a slow song came on from indoors, Michele asked me to dance. Dancing close, he leaned down and kissed me.

Giddy just by being in his arms, I just stood there holding my breath. Even after the song had ended, we both stood there swaying back and forth. Neither of us wanted to let the other out of our arms.

So that was my first experience with love. I'd never known the definition of "romance"—until this night. But surely this was it. For me, it was better than any romance novel I'd ever read; better than any love movie I'd ever seen.

But just as the song ended, so did this night. I've never seen Michele again. But I'll never forget him. They say you never forget your first love. I'm sure of it.

—Shire Feingold, 16

They Call Us "The Cutest Couple at School"

He was the model boyfriend: smart, friendly and courteous.

—Tara Cutshaw, 18

In my junior year my family moved from Palm Springs to Washington State, then to Carlsbad, California, where I finally settled into yet a third high school. With no friends—once again—I was lonely and, quite frankly, tired of being the "new girl." I was really looking forward to having friends, and a boyfriend! Everyone, it seemed, had love in their lives. I didn't even have friends, except for my sister—who was not only in love but engaged and getting married!

As soon as I settled in this new school, I looked around to see if any of the boys had potential. There were a few, but wouldn't you know all the good-looking ones were taken! Always on the lookout for love, I couldn't help but notice a couple who seemed perfect for each other. Peter and Janis were so cute together. Everyone liked them and referred to them as "the cutest couple at school." Whenever I saw either of them, sure enough, there was the other. Janis was adorable, but Peter, well, not only was Peter nice looking, but he was the model boyfriend: smart, friendly and courteous.

Peter became my ideal. I really wanted a boyfriend like Peter. But I knew I'd have to "pay my dues." How was I going to find my Prince Peter Charming if I didn't get involved in school activities? I started being "social." This led to my going out with Michael, a nice guy, but well, it was more boring than watching grass grow. I did go out a few times with other guys, but my heart never really came along.

The year came to an end—and surprisingly, so did Peter and Janis's relationship.

My senior year started, and I began dating someone who was nice, but I couldn't get Peter off my mind. Much to my surprise, Peter was in three of my classes. We got to know each other and started talking. A good friend of mine, Jodie, was best friends with Peter (I'm pretty sure she secretly had a crush on him), but luckily, she had met a new guy, Nathan, and the two of them really clicked. As it turned out, Nathan was also a good friend of Peter's. This was just great because it meant the four of us could hang out together and really enjoy our time together as a foursome. Jodie talked to Peter about me, and I talked to Nathan about Jodie, and everything was going well. For the homecoming dance, Peter asked me, and Nathan asked Jodie at the same time. That's when things started to heat up. To make a long story short, Peter and I have been going out for a while now. Nathan and Jodie are still going out, too! If someone were to tell me oh-so-many months ago that my boyfriend was going be Peter, I would never have believed it.

We're getting ready to graduate now and know that the future—and the way we feel about each other—is something we still must discuss. What we've decided is that we hope to be in each other's lives, if not forever, then at least for a long, long time. Peter wants to go to a college out of state, and I want to stay home and attend a college here in town for a few years then possibly transfer somewhere closer to him. I hope that our love will last our lifetimes. I feel that it can. But I also know that the years ahead will have their challenging times as well. I talk with friends who are in college, and many of them have been through the situation I'm facing. Not too many relationships survive when couples go to separate schools. I know it will be hard. Still, my heart tells me that I am willing to do what I can to see if our relationship can be a forever one. Only time will tell. I do know that I've never cared for anyone so much before.

So that's my experience with "true love." I couldn't have been more surprised by "who" came into my life. Nor could I have been more surprised by how much we loved and cared for and about each other. But love is that way; you really don't know what is in store for you. And that's the exciting part. You just must believe that love will come into your life—even if you don't know when. Once there, you must trust that there is a reason for its being—even if in the beginning you aren't exactly sure what that is. And you must trust that however it transforms—however it changes—you will be accepting of it.

I believe, you just must treat it like a gift, a gift that comes from a sacred place. And sometimes that is enough. As for Peter and me, we trust that whatever the future holds, is right for the two of us.

—**Sara Cutshaw, 18**

How Do You Know—for Sure—If It's Love at First Sight?

My girlfriend and I were driving around, and she needed gas. We turned into a 7–11. While she pumped gas, I went into the store to get us Cokes. A cute guy was in the checkout lane in front of me, fumbling in his pockets for money. Either he was short a dime or he was flirting, because when he noticed me behind him, he smiled nice and then asked, "Do you by chance have a dime I can borrow?"

My heart fluttering, I dug around the bottom of my purse for a dime, found one and handed it over. He paid for his things and then handed me a pen and his receipt saying, "Give me your phone number. Maybe we can hang out sometime." "Sure, okay," I said, happily writing down my name and number for him. "Great!" he said, smiling. It wasn't until I'd watched him disappear that I realized in my nervousness, I'd forgotten to ask him his name. For the next week I waited by the phone. No call.

Two weeks passed—still no call. Four weeks later, still no call. I've even gone back to that same 7–11 hoping I'd see him but haven't. So that's it. Short and sweet. Well, short at least. I don't recommend waiting by the phone, especially when you don't even know the name of the person you're expecting a call from.

I'm not sure if what I felt was "love at first sight," or if it was just my imagination. I do know, however, that the experience was worth the ten cents!

—**Monica Wells, 15**

No Matter What Your Age, Being Dumped Hurts

I never really knew how much it hurt to be "left" until a girlfriend of five months dumped me. Man, did my heart hurt. In fact, it just ached. So that got me to thinking about how my mother must have felt when my dad left her for another woman. When that happened, Mom cried and cried. I was really upset, too, but my feelings were more about anger than tears. Not having any experience in "losing" at love prior to when my girlfriend left me, I'd say that I really couldn't empathize with my mom as she went through the separation and divorce ordeal.

It might even be fair to say that I was angry with her—thinking if she'd done something different, then she and Dad wouldn't be splitting up. But looking back, now that I know what a broken heart feels like, I can see that my mother was heartbroken. And what a terrible time that must have been for her. Because now I do know how that feels.

So that's probably the biggest lesson I've learned about love: how it hurts to have your heart broken. But what I don't understand is how someone can leave a person he once loved so passionately. I mean, how is it possible to fall out of love so fast? Just one week before my girlfriend left me, she told me she loved me. And I'm positive that my parents must have been very much in love at one time.

What I least understand about love is why it's not a more permanent thing. I mean, if you choose someone for all the right reasons, then why can't it last? If love is really that fickle, then how can you ever know for sure if you're choosing the right person?

One thing is for sure: No matter what your age, it hurts when love ends.

—Crane Adams, 17

What Proof Do You Have That He Loves You?

What I've learned about love is that you can give away too much of yourself. It's been my experience that when you do that, it changes things, and not always for the best. As a result of trusting someone's words, "I love you," I went too far.

I'd never do that again. I believe that a few guys—not all guys—will say almost anything to get you to go all the way with them.

I think that when a guy tells you he loves you, before you fall head-over-heels in love with him, you should make him prove he loves you. Ask him to ask you for a date (as opposed to just meeting him somewhere). Ask him to pick you up from your house and to ask your parents what time they expect him to bring you home.

How he responds will be good "proof" of how much he loves you. Try it. You'll see.

—Jalette Daye, 17

What Does It Mean When a Girl Calls You a "Bad Boyfriend"?

A girl I really liked, and thought was special told me I was a "bad boyfriend." I don't know what that means. Nor do I have any idea what I did (or didn't do) to deserve being labeled as such.

I don't want to be a bad boyfriend, but what is a "bad boyfriend"? I did ask her, but she told me if I had to ask, I was "too dense" and therefore not worth the explanation.

The next girlfriend I had I treated really, nice. I wanted to make sure I did everything just right. After going out for two months, she told me I was boring. So, I'm confused.

I'd say that right now I'm not exactly sure how girls want a guy to act, but I want to know. Right now, I don't have a girlfriend—but I want one. Probably I should get girls figured out first—which is a difficult thing to do because they all act so differently.

I'd say I don't really understand love just yet. Or maybe I just don't understand girls.

—Danny Power, 16

Love Can Complicate Your Life

I'm in love. I consider my boyfriend my high school sweetheart. I've been going out with him since I was a freshman. My parents like him, and his parents like me.

Having a boyfriend has its advantages and disadvantages. It's great to feel you love someone and to know that person loves you. Even so, I sometimes I think I am too young to be committed to one person.

I think a relationship is a lot of work. Even though I can't imagine being without my boyfriend; I realize that depend on him to make me happy. Like when I'm without him, I feel unhappy. Or if we have an argument, then my heart aches and I'm sad, and feel incredibly out of balance.

I also find that even being as much in love as I am makes me feel "out of balance." I find myself really wanting to be with my boyfriend, and then when I do spend a lot of time with him, I feel like I need some space. And having a boyfriend doesn't mean your loneliness goes away. Sometimes I feel lonely, even when I'm with him. And what else troubles me is that I want him to want to date just me—still, I sometimes want to date others. But I don't want him to be free to date others.

What I've learned most about love is that it is not the answer to everything. That's a real eye-opener because when everyone has a boyfriend except you,

you think that everyone is happier and has a better time than you. But then you get a boyfriend, and you find that while, yes, it's wonderful to be in love, it's only one thing—and not your whole life. Does that make sense?

I guess I'm saying that I thought when I had a boyfriend, life would be better. It's not. In fact, I'd say having a boyfriend makes things complicated.

—**Maria Diona, 17**

I Dream About You Every Night

I dream about you every night
Each one the same
I try to imagine everything about you
Yet I know nothing but your name.

I find a table in the cafeteria
Where I stare from across the room
Watch as you laugh and talk with friends
Bigger than life you loom.

You seem like such a cool girl
Perfect in every way
Could it happen between us?
Will I find the words to say?

Night and day I dream the dream
There is a you, me and an "us"
I'm wishing, hoping and wanting this
In a clandestine vision I put my trust.

I dream about us on a date
And sharing a good-night kiss
I see us at the homecoming dance
You're holding me close; it's bliss.

I dream about us doing homework
Sharing moments washing my car
We're in the show ring at the fair

I hope such times are near, not far.

I see us going steady
Laughing and holding hands as we walk along
You've got your arms around me
As we sing to our favorite song.

I dream about us hanging out
Talking and laughing as natural as we might
Kicking back, laying in the park together
Making plans for sweetly promised nights.

I dream about you every night,
Each one the same
I imagine that I know everything about you
Yet I know nothing but your name.

—**Sean Sanders, 16**

To Dance with the Man in the Moon

I close my eyes and dream of a place
Where sadness doesn't exist
Harm isn't a real word
And tears come only from happiness.

I close my eyes and dream of a place
Where stars are the floor to heaven,
A place where young and old can live
And wishes are granted in lots of seven.

I close my eyes and dream of a place
Where love is the only currency needed
Where thoughts and notions are all evolved
And flowerbeds are forever seeded.

I close my eyes and dream of a place
Where I can dance arm in arm with the man in
the moon
And the wind can have a conversation with me
And the sun shines at the sound of a tune.

I close my eyes and dream of a place
A world where people are rooting for each other
Knowing that if we wanted—you, me, each of us
In a heartbeat, together, we could create it.

—Angelina Cardinale, 19

Blonde Girl . . . Big Feet

Who am I to you, God . . .
. . . blonde girl with big feet
. . . her dad's eyes and
. . . her mom's smile?
Is it that simple to you?
Is it supposed to be a complicated top secret to
me?
If so, you've succeeded
Because
I feel confusion
Over who I am versus who I can be
I'm so filled with conflicting ideals
. . . the good versus the bad,
Always doing battle
. . . conscience versus matter
A questioning mind,
. . . an unsure heart
Always running into
. . . the wall to my soul
. . . the mysteries of heart
Is that the plan, God,
. . . that it be a secret to me?
Or wait . . .
It's not about me . . . but rather, YOU . . .
Are you watching me play . . .
. . . play out who you've destined me to be?

—Heather McHale, 17

Barbies, Boys and Malls

From dress-up and dolls
To boys and malls,
You're the finest friend of all
You've been that special someone when I needed
to spill it all.

We've talked about our dreams for the future
Sorted and categorized our fears
Schemed how to break curfew and a few rules,
Held each other through alligator tears.

I'm so glad to have been in these "places" with
you
Best friends for so many incredible years
More than a good friend, you are the sister I
never had,
We squabble, share clothes and work through
being mad.

Though our world of Barbie and make-believe
is gone
And college days and adult times lay just ahead
Husbands, kids, careers may come and go,
But we'll stay best friends forever, till the end.

—Cassandra Kollath, 17

Should I Take You Back?

Did I make a mistake to leave you
Should I take you back
Would that be wise or foolish
Do I need to cut you a little slack?

So much happened, so much went down
Yet you love me . . . and I love you
But how can I forget what happened?
We did things we shouldn't do.

And how do I trust you now?
It was you who shut that door
I let many, many things go . . .
And then finally couldn't ignore.

Two broken and now regretting hearts
Was it worth it—for sure it wasn't fair
I'm so disappointed that we've broken up
I know that we both still care.

Now here we are trying to be "just friends"
And we can if we're standing ten miles apart . .
. A
s long as we're not in each other's sight . . .
It's the only way I can control my aching heart.

We went to the movies as "just two friends"
You sat close; our hands touched; didn't realize

I cared so much
  A total journey back in time . . .
  If I didn't tell a single friend of mine.

  So very conflicted but what am I to do
  Like when you came to see me the very next day
  You asked if I was surprised to see you . . .
  I love you but with all that is between us, what
am I to say?

  I'm involved with someone new now
  I can't forget yet I need to move on
  My feelings for you so deep, yet hidden away
  But I still cry when I hear our song.

  He makes me smile and I need that,
  So, I'm giving the new guy a chance
  Need to forget about everything—especially you
  It's hard; nothing compares to our romance.

  So, two still-in-love hearts will be moving on,
  Telling ourselves we'll be just friends
  Will we succeed in that or will we find
  That two hearts in love can never end?
                              —Kacey Stepanek, 17

Scandalous Mementos

Mildew in the air
Gleaming dust hanging in the light
There in a grimy box of brown photos
My teenaged father looks up at me
Sporting bangs nearly to his eyes
Most assuredly scandalous at the time.

College memorabilia
A sweater proudly bearing
Bold letters of their alma mater
They fell in love there
A picture of them cuddling
Under a tree makes me smile.

And now photos of years later
Still cuddling on their Golden Anniversary
beneath a lovely weeping willow
I can hear their comfortable laughter, but then
A huge silence seizes the room, a reminder of how
much I miss them
Taking comfort in knowing they share an eternal
bed.

A fatal twist of metal
Stole any hope of a normal life from me
At such an early age, I had no guide
They left too fast for me to say it
So, I repeat the words endlessly

To lifeless mementos of your beautiful life.

Never blinking, while tears fall down
I consider my life and what it's become
What shall I do without you until the day?
My life becomes photographs and sweaters
The day I join you under the willow
And tell you in person, "You left too soon"?
                                    —Tom Hatfield, 17

Who Teaches Guys to Smile That Way?

I love it when you smile
The way you always do
It's the one that makes me melt,
And gives me something to hold onto.

I love it when you grip my hand
Can it mean there'll never be heartbreak or tears?
Or that whenever I'm lonely, worried or insecure
That you'll chase away ill-tempered fears?

I love the way you hold me
Like I'm a china doll of glass
So afraid you'll hurt or break me
Like I'm precious and first-class.

I love the way you kiss me
On the hands, lips and cheek
I think about it day and night
Even thoughts make knees go weak.

I love the way my heart feels
When you glance at me in that special way
It seems to say a million things
Is it merely amusement, or does it imply you'll
stay?

So many things I love about you
From your nose down to your toes

But if you want to know how to get to me
It's all about the way you hold me close.

Spectacular is how I'd describe your smile
The one the best guys always do
It always makes me melt and lets me know
I'm going to hold onto you.

—Morgan Redding, 14

Only One

We're all lost,
We're all found,
We're all the same.
Just one heart
With different names.

—Laura Campanelli, 20

Anticipated Night

Dress shopping hours on end
Finding the perfect one.
Shoes to match.
Purse to match.
Nails to match,
Hair appointment to schedule and keep,
Place an order and pick up the boutonniere,
Change clothes,
Find your shoes,
An hour for makeup,
Get ready.
Excitement,
Joy,
Nervousness,
All the same.
Waiting, waiting
Anxiously.
Here he comes.
The doorbell rings.
Heart beating fast,
Black shirt, silver tie,
Very classy.
Looking great.
Off we go, homecoming dance
What a night—
. . . One I've been waiting for!

—Kylie Lynn, 16

CHAPTER 3

Understanding Feelings of Love:
Your Personal Workbook

*Love is the irresistible desire
to be irresistibly desired.*
—**Robert Frost**

What do you think poet Robert Frost had in mind when he penned this quote?

_____

_____

Do you think the desire to be irresistibly desired is a universal feeling, felt by everyone, young and old alike, or that not everyone has a need to experience love in this way?

_____

_____

_____

In what way do you feel "irresistibly desired" by your mom and dad?

_____

In what way would your parents say that they feel irresistibly desired by you?

_____

_____

Who besides your family loves you?

_____

How does it feel (or how do you think it feels) to be, in Robert Frost's words, "irresistibly desired"?

_____

_____

What is the best thing about feeling love?

_____

_____

Are you in love with anyone? Is anyone in love with you?

_____

_____

The Power of Love in Our Lives

Being loved affirms that we are lovable, worth loving. Giving love gives us purpose: we are needed.

What does this quote mean to you?

_____

_____

Love has been called the most potent force in all the world. There's no greater force for good, no greater power for creating change in our lives.

What does this quote mean to you?

_____

_____

How does being a loving person act as a "force for good" in your life? For example, does it make you more patient, more tolerant, more forgiving, more open-minded? How does it "color" the way you see yourself and others?

_____

_____

Do you think if we all do our part to "love enough" that we could make the world an even better place in which to live?

_____

_____

Do you think people the world over are showing more love and tolerance for each other more than they did, say, three years ago? Why?

_____

_____

Being a Loving Person

What do you think is the difference between being a "loving" person and being a "lovable" person?

_____

_____

All that matters is what we do for each other.

—Lewis Carroll

Who Was Your First Love?

Who was your first love? What was it that made that person so special?

_____

_____

How did you know it was "love" you were feeling? What were the signs?

_____

_____

How did you meet that person? Where did you meet? How old were you? How old was he or she? Is that person still your love?

_____

_____

Did your friends like this person? How do you know? What did they say that makes you feel this way?

_____

_____

Did your parents approve? How do you know? What did they say?

_____

_____

I used to be shy. You made me sing.

—Rumi

What does this quote mean to you?

_____

_____

A Tete-a-Tete with Your Heart

Do you ever "talk" with your heart? Write a letter to your heart, thanking it for all the love it brings into your life. Tell your heart how you would like it to "behave" in matters of love!

My Dear Heart,

_____

_____

_____

_____

———————————————————

———————————————————

———————————————————

———————————————————

———————————————————

———————————————————

Write about a time you liked someone, and it felt just right to your heart. Who was that someone? How did your heart know it was right—how did you feel at the time?

———————————————————

———————————————————

———————————————————

CHOICES: Should You Listen to Your Heart, or Head?

The heart is forever inexperienced in love.

—Henry David Thoreau

What do you think this quote means? How has it been true or not true for you?

_____

_____

The Best Thing About Love . . .

What is the best thing about having a special someone in your life?

_____

_____

What do your friends think about that person?

_____

_____

What do your parents think about that person?

_____

_____

In the story " How Far I'll Go" found in Chapter Two in this book, 17 year-old Christopher Gillian describes "how far" he went for love. What conclusions did he eventually draw about the relationship?

_____

_____

Have you ever "gone too far" for love? How?

_____

_____

Write about a time when you made a decision to do something for love, and you went too far. What did you do? Who was involved? What were your feelings at the time?

_____

_____

How did things turn out? What happened? How do you feel about the whole thing now? What did you learn from the experience?

_____

_____

_____

_____

If you could do one thing over in the entire experience, what would it be?

_____

_____

Decisions: "How Far" Will You Go for Love?

List five things that are so important to you that you will not "sacrifice" for love, for example, your spiritual beliefs, your values, or your time with family and friends. Tell why each is important to you.

1. What I won't sacrifice and why: _____

_____

2. What I won't sacrifice and why: _____

_____

3. What I won't sacrifice and why: _____

_____

4. What I won't sacrifice and why: _____

_____

5. What I won't sacrifice and why: _____

_____

What is your commitment for staying true to yourself even in the face of pressure to do otherwise?

_____

_____

What Is "Unconditional Love"?

Unconditional love means accepting someone for who he or she is and loving that person in spite of his or her shortcomings. It means believing in and loving that person "no matter what." Yet, we wouldn't allow ourselves to stay in a relationship if it wasn't healthy for us to do so. Loving unconditionally can even mean letting someone go.

What does "unconditional love" mean to you?

_____

_____

Name two people who *love you* unconditionally, and how you know they do.

1. Who:_____

   How I know it: _____

   _____

2. Who:_____

How I know it: _____

_____

Love is what you've been through
with somebody.

—James Thurber

What does this quote mean to you?

_____

_____

_____

DECISIONS: Letting Go, Moving On

A thousand half-loves must be
forsaken to take one whole heart
home.

—Rumi

What do you think this quote means?

_____

_____

Write about a time when you knew a relationship was just not good for you, and so you had to say no to the friendship. Why was the relationship not a good choice for you? Who did you have to "let go"?

_____

_____

_____

How long had you known this person before you realized the friendship wasn't right for you? Was it an easy decision to make or was it difficult? What was the easiest part? What was the difficult part?

_____

_____

_____

Did you make the decision alone, or did your friends or parents encourage you to "let go"? What did someone else do that was helpful to you in "letting go"?

_____

_____

_____

How did the other person know you were "letting go" of being in the relationship? Did you tell the person, or did your friends, or did he or she just know you were not committed to being friends any longer?

_____

_____

How did he or she feel about your desire to "move on"? What did he or she say?

_____

_____

_____

How do you feel about your decision? How do you feel about yourself for having made the decision?

_____

_____

DECISIONS: Loving Someone Special

I love you because I know you so well; I love you in spite of knowing you so well!

What do you think this phrase means?

_____

_____

Do you love anyone "in spite of knowing" that person? Who? Why do you love that person?

_____

_____

Does anyone love you "in spite of knowing you so well"? Who? How do you know?

_____

_____

Nothing can match the treasure of common memories, of trials endured together, of quarrels and reconciliations and generous emotions.
—**Antoine De Saint-Exupery**

How does this quote fit your family experience?

_____

_____

The first places we experience love is in our homes. The love of our parents and other family members is expressed in many ways—hugs and kisses, encouragement, and attention to the things that help us grow up in healthy ways.

List five of the nicest things the members of your family do for you:

1. Who:_____

   Expression of love: _____

   _____

2. Who:_____

   Expression of love: _____

   _____

3. Who:_____

   Expression of love: _____

   _____

4. Who:_____

   Expression of love: _____

   _____

5. Who:_____

   Expression of love: _____

   _____

What Do You Do to Show Your Family You Love Them?

List five of the nicest things you do for the members of your family that shows them you love and appreciate each of them.

1. Who:_____

   Expression of love: _____

   _____

2. Who:_____

   Expression of love: _____

   _____

3. Who:_____

   Expression of love: _____

   _____

4. Who:_____

   Expression of love: _____

   _____

5. Who:_____

   Expression of love: _____

   _____

If you could add three more things to your list, what would they be?

❤ _____

❤ _____

❤ _____

Why aren't you doing these things now? How do you think it will make your family feel when you start doing them?

_____

_____

_____

_____

Bonds of the Heart: Loving Your Family

Write about an incident your family has been through together that made you feel really close to each other. For example, maybe your parents divorced or you lost a family pet and each of you comforted the other during these times. Maybe it was a time you took a special vacation and everyone had such a good time. What was the circumstance? What happened? In what ways did you come together?

_____

_____

_____

_____

_____

How did the incident cause you to care about the members of your family even more? In what ways are you closer now? How does that make you feel?

_____

_____

_____

When you and your parents aren't seeing eye to eye, how does it make you feel? How does it affect you? For example, does it make you irritable with your friends, teachers and others? Do you get quiet, feel sad or get teary?

_____

_____

_____

How do you express those feelings? For example, do you go to your room and want to be left alone, or do you want to talk about it right away? Do you try to "punish" your parents by pouting, or do you try to get on their good side by doing nice things, such as taking it upon yourself to vacuum or do some other chore without being asked?

_____

_____

_____

When you and your parents are in a "good place," how does it make you feel? How does it affect you? For example, are you happier when you are with your friends, teachers and others?

_____

_____

_____

How do you express those feelings? For example, are you more talkative, sharing more with them about what's going on in your life? Do you tell them "I love you" and "thank you" more often than usual?

_____

_____

_____

LOVE LESSONS:
Did Someone You Love, Leave?

Snowy Bird

I was visiting a bird sanctuary, when in the distance, I spotted a young man with a white bird on his fingers. As he moved the bird up and down, the bird got into the spirit of things, lifting his little wings up and down in perfect rhythm with the man's movements. The man gave a little signal, and the bird began to swing around the man's fingers, as if a circus acrobat.

Enchanted, I walked closer to see the beautiful white bird perched on the finger of the attendant. "Marty," his name badge read.

"Hi, Marty," I said. "Great bird. What is it?"

"This is Snowy Bird," Marty replied. "He's an umbrella cockatoo." The cockatoo was snow white in color, a regal-looking bird with a high plume of feathers fanning from the crown of his head. But there was one exception to his majestic appearance—Snowy Bird had no feathers on his chest. Jarred by seeing this beautiful and obviously talented bird with such a raw and featherless chest, I asked Marty, "What happened? Did he have mites?"

Marty shook his head and explained, "No, Snowy Bird plucks out all the feathers on his chest himself. You see, two years ago his owners had to move out of the state and felt they could no longer care for him, so they brought their bird here. Snowy Bird is heartbroken. He still hasn't stopped pining for them. One of the ways he mourns them is to pluck the feathers from his chest."

And he still hasn't gotten over it?" I asked, feeling for this beautiful little bird with a heartache.

"Apparently not," Marty explained. "Whatever it is that goes on in Snowy Bird's head or heart, he is still missing them."

Love, so important—to all of us. Even to umbrella cockatoos, especially one by the name of Snowy Bird who pines to bring back a love and closeness he once knew.

—Bettie Jean Burres

Did someone you love ever leave you? Who? Why did that person leave? How did their leaving make you feel?

_____

_____

Write about a time you were heartbroken. What happened? Who was involved? How did you feel about it?

_____

_____

_____

Did your heart heal or is it still hurting? When your heart is hurting, how do you comfort it?

_____

_____

_____

Where you used to be there is a hole in the world.
—**Edna St. Vincent Millay**

Have you ever felt these words? Who left a "hole" in your world? Why?

_____

_____

_____

"It's the absolute pits to have a huge crush on someone who just sees you as a friend—or worse yet, who doesn't even know you're alive."
—**Heather Liston, 16**

How have you experienced this quote? What happened? How did this make you feel? How did it turn out in the end?

_____

_____

What did you learn from going through the hurt? How did your heartbreak help you become wiser? How do you put that wisdom to use?

_____

_____

_____

_____

_____

Loving Yourself Is the Greatest Love of All

Though we like to think we can handle almost anything, our hearts are still sensitive and fragile. So we have to remember to handle them with care. One of the most important things we do in life is learn to love ourselves.

What do you think it means to take care of your heart?

_____

_____

_____

How do you show your love for yourself?

_____

_____

_____

List three things you can do to be good to yourself when your heart is hurting:

❤ _____

❤ _____

❤ _____

3 Wishes for Love in My Life

If a fairy godmother granted you three wishes for having love in your life, what would you ask for?

Dear Fairy Godmother,

➤ Wish # 1: _____

_____

_____

➤ Wish # 2: _____

_____

_____

➤ Wish # 3_____

_____

_____

Loving the World We Live In

Without opening your door, you can open your heart to the world.

—Tao Te Ching

What do you think this quote means?

_____

_____

Earth—a "Tiny Blue Marble"

In December 1999, Steve Smith, veteran of three space flights, over three-hundred Earth orbits and five space walks, was a crew member of the space shuttle Discovery, who during an eight-hour-long

Christmas Eve walk in Space, repaired the Hubble Space Telescope. This is what he said about how earth looks from space.

From space, the Earth looks like a tiny blue marble lying in an endless black ocean. The Earth appears so small, so fragile, and yet it is our home, one that supports and sustains many forms of life.

As I gaze at our Earth home from space, I am filled with awe for it, and I know that life is sacred. We must each care deeply. Looking out for each other and our Earth home is an act of love. Pay attention to the things going on around you. In the bigger scheme of things, even things that may seem small and insignificant are vital to a healthy Earth and to healthy people. Do your part.

Ironically, it was seeing how small our planet appeared in the very vastness of this universe that filled me with the greatest sense of love for it.

— Astronaut Steve Smith

When you read his thoughts about viewing the earth from space, how does it make you feel? In what way do you love "Mother Earth?

_____

_____

Love asks us to protect all life as sacred. When we value this connection we show our love and appreciation for our Mother Earth by protecting our environment.

Three Wishes . . .

You've been given the power to grant Mother Earth three wishes. What do you think Mother Earth would wish for? For example, do you think she would want all her endangered species to be protected, or do you think she would want all her people to be at peace, or would she want all her rivers to be clean again? What are her three greatest wishes and why would you choose each for her?

🌎 Wish # 1: _____

_____

_____

🌎 Wish # 2: _____

_____

_____

🌎 Wish # 3 _____

_____

_____

We live in a world that needs love.

What does this saying mean to you?

_____

_____

_____

How Your Brain Decides If You Will Become Addicted—Or Not

Information and Encouragement for Teens, with Stories by Teens and Young Adults
Jennifer Leigh Youngs, A.A. | Bettie B. Youngs, Ph.D., Ed.D.

- *"using," dependency and addiction*
- *if you or a friend can't stop using*
- *Withdrawal, Relapse, and Recovery*
- *cool ways to say "no"*

Book: 978-1-940784-99-1
e-book: 978-1-940784-98-4

Setting and Achieving Goals that Matter to ME

Information and Encouragement for Teens, with Stories by Teens
Jennifer Leigh Youngs, A.A. | Bettie B. Youngs, Ph.D., Ed.D.

- *discovering what's important TO ME*
- *hobbies, talents, interests, apptitudes*
- *hopes, aspirations and dreaming big*
- *my goal-setting workbook*

Book: 978-1-940784-97-7
e-book: 978-1-940784-96-0

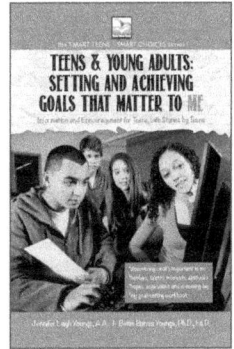

Managing Stress, Pressure, and the Ups and Downs of Life

Information, Encouragement and Inspiration—with commentary by teens
Jennifer Leigh Youngs, A.A. | Bettie B. Youngs, Ph.D., Ed.D.

- *great ways to manage stress and pressure*
- *how stress works for—and against—you*
- *physical, emotional and behavioral signs of stress*
- *staying cool under pressure*

Book: 978-1-940784-80-9
e-book: 978-1-940784-81-6

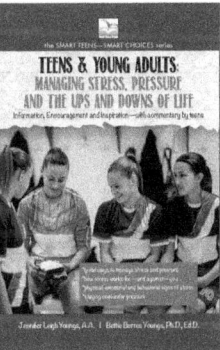

The 10 Commandments and the Secret Each One Guards—For You

Information and Inspirational Short Stories
Bettie B. Youngs, Ph.D., Ed.D. | Jennifer Leigh Youngs, A.A.

- *how the Commandments speak to you*
- *the secret each Commandment guards*
- *using your faith to guide the choices you make*
- *how to be confident and bold in your faith*

Book: 978-1-940784-95-3
e-book: 978-1-940784-94-6

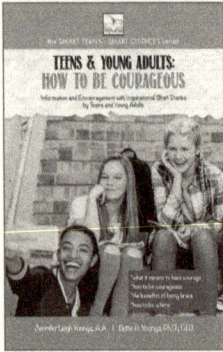

How to Be Courageous

Encouragment and Inspirational Short Stories by Teens and Young Adults
Jennifer Leigh Youngs, A.A. | Bettie B. Youngs, Ph.D., Ed.D.

- *the importance of being courageous*
- *the benefits of being brave*
- *how to be a hero*

Book: 978-1-940784-93-9
e-book: 978-1-940784-92-2

Growing Your Confidence and Self-Esteem

Information, Encouragement and Inspirational Short Stories by Teens and Young Adults
Jennifer Leigh Youngs, A.A. | Bettie B. Youngs, Ph.D., Ed.D.

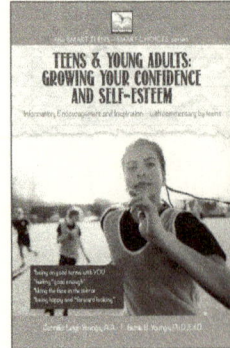

- *being on good terms with YOU*
- *feeling "good enough"*
- *the power of confience*
- *liking the face in the mirror*
- *being happy and "forward looking"*

Book: 978-1-940784-86-1
e-book: 978-1-940784-87-8

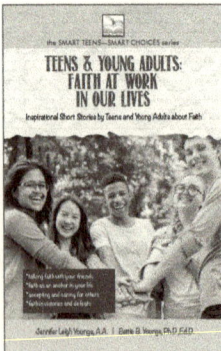

Faith at Work in Our Lives

Information, Encouragement and Inspirational Short Stories by Teens and Young Adults
Jennifer Leigh Youngs, A.A. | Bettie B. Youngs, Ph.D., Ed.D.

- *talking faith with your friends*
- *faith as an anchor in your life*
- *accepting and caring for others*
- *faith in victories and defeats*

Book: 978-1-940784-78-6
e-book: 978-1-940784-79-3

Understanding Feelings of Love

Inspirational Short Stories by Teens and Young Adults
Jennifer Leigh Youngs, A.A. | Bettie B. Youngs, Ph.D., Ed.D.

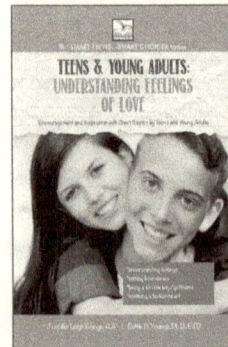

- *the lessons of love*
- *setting boundaries important to you*
- *4 ways to be a great boy/girlfriend*
- *when love relationships end*

Book: 978-1-940784-75-5
e-book: 978-1-940784-74-8

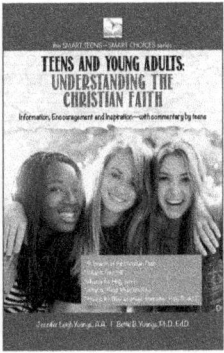

Understanding the Christian Faith

Information, Encouragement and Inspirational Short Stories by Teens and Young Adults

Jennifer Leigh Youngs, A.A. | Bettie B. Youngs, Ph.D., Ed.D.

- *9 Tenants of the Christian Faith*
- *What is Free Will*
- *What is the Holly Spirit*
- *What is "Reap What You Sow"*
- *How is the Bible as unique from other Holy Books?*

Book: 978-1-940784-76-2
e-book: 978-1-940784-77-9

How to be a Good Friend

Information and Encouragement with Inspirational Short Stories
by Teens and Young Adults

Jennifer Leigh Youngs, A.A. | Bettie B. Youngs, Ph.D., Ed.D.

- *understanding friendships*
- *how to be a good friend*
- *making, keeping, and ending friendships*
- *mending hurt feelings*

Book: 978-1-940784-73-1
e-book: 978-1-940784-72-4

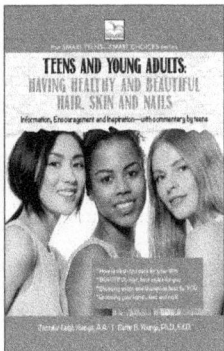

Having Healthy and Beautiful Hair, Skin and Nails

Information, Encouragement and Inspiration—with commentary by teens

Jennifer Leigh Youngs, A.A. | Bettie B. Youngs, Ph.D., Ed.D.

- *how to clean and care for your skin*
- *BEAUTIFUL hair; best styles for you*
- *choosing soaps and shampoos best for YOU*
- *grooming your hands, feet, and nails*

Book: 978-1-940784-84-7
e-book: 978-1-940784-85-4

The Power of Being Kind, Courteous and Thoughtful

Information, Encouragement and Inspirational Short Stories by Teens and Young Adults

Jennifer Leigh Youngs, A.A. | Bettie B. Youngs, Ph.D., Ed.D.

- *the power of being KIND*
- *the importance of being COURTEOUS*
- *how to be "THOUGHTFUL"*

Book: 978-1-940784-82-3
e-book: 978-1-940784-83-0

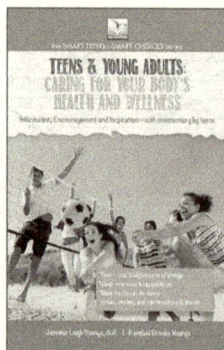

www.ingramcontent.com/pod-product-compliance
Lightning Source LLC
Chambersburg PA
CBHW032103080426
42733CB00006B/392